THE GREAT
DEPRESSION
A Nation In Distress

Contributing Editors
Janet Beyer and JoAnne B. Weisman

Discovery Enterprises, Ltd.
Carlisle, Massachusetts

© Discovery Enterprises, Ltd., Carlisle, MA 1995
ISBN 1-878668-46-3 paperback edition
Library of Congress Catalog Card Number 95-68771

10   9   8   7   6   5   4   3

Printed in the United States of America

Subject Reference Guide

The Great Depression: A Nation in Distress
Contributing editors Janet Beyer and JoAnne B. Weisman
Introduced by Kenneth M. Deitch

The Great Depression — U.S. History
The 1930s — U.S. History
Herbert Hoover — U.S. Presidents

Photo/Illustration Credits

Front page of the *New York Times,* October 30, 1929 (p.8)

Bank in Haverhill, Iowa (p. 20); shopfronts, Vicksburg, Mississippi (p. 27);
Post Office, Nethers, Virginia (p. 49); Cider stand, Blue Ridge Mountains,
Virginia (p. 51); Ozark cabin, Missouri (p. 53); farmer and son, Cimarron
County, Oklahoma (p. 56); and fruit workers from Tennessee (p. 60).
Photos reproduced from the Collection of the Library of Congress.

Front page of June, 1938 edition Action Comics No. 1 (p. 42).
Courtesy of Detective Comics, Inc.

Excerpts/Reprints

(pp. 23-26), courtesy of *Fortune* magazine.

Table of Contents

Introduction...5
by Kenneth M. Deitch

Economic Distress.. 15
Hoover's Early Warning
Hoover Urges Banking Reform
Taking Action

"No One Has Starved" 23
Excerpt from Fortune *magazine article*
The Discovery of Poverty
Hooverville
Southern Negroes Felt the Depression Later
Beans, Bacon, and Gravy
The Bonus Expeditionary Force
Letters from the Forgotten Man

Entertainment to Lighten the Heart...................................... 39
Who's Afraid of the Big Bad Wolf? By Janet Beyer
Brother, Can You Spare A Dime?
Ideal Women
A Super Hero

The Women Get Involved 43
"Pocketbook Patriotism"
The Women's Emergency Brigade at Flint, Michigan
Dorothy Day and the Bread Lines

The Face of the People.. 49
Farm Life
And If You Were Sick...
The Dust Bowl
Grasshoppers and Dust

Searching For Hope.. 59
The Country Migrates
200,000 Vagabond Children
The Joad Family Joins the Westward Migration
Looking Ahead to Better Times, by JoAnne B. Weisman

Suggestions for Further Reading 64

A Word About the Contributors... 64

Introduction

by
Kenneth M. Deitch

What is a depression? It is one of the phases that an economy can go through. If an economy contracts sufficiently from a condition of prosperity, it enters what is called a recession. If the deterioration goes enough further, the economy passes beyond recession into depression. A depression is a phase in which the level of economic activity is short of its potential by a gaping margin.

Because no one can "see" an entire economy, we rely on statistical indicators to learn its condition at a particular moment. One of the most carefully monitored among these indicators is the percentage of the labor force that is unemployed. As a depression is popularly understood, it is a phase characterized by persistent, massive, and widespread unemployment. In assessing a particular economy at a given moment, experts might differ on whether it is in a recession or a depression, but for America in the 1930s, there can be no doubt.

It is beyond the scope of this book to explain what causes depressions, but two introductory—and interrelated—points should be made. First, the American economy entered the 1930s with certain institutional flaws that contributed to the depression. Over the subsequent decades, many steps have been taken to reduce them. The creation of the Securities and Exchange Commission to provide general supervision over trading in securities markets is but one important example. Second, market economies inevitably experience fluctuations. Prior to the mid-1930s, their causes were not well understood. Just around then, they started becoming so. The pioneering work was done by a brilliant British economist named John Maynard Keynes in his

book *The General Theory of Employment Interest and Money.*
Keynes is the central creative figure in the development of modern
"macroeconomics," the study of the economy in the large. Periods
of recession are still with us, but because of the contributions of
Keynes and many who followed him, the danger that there will be
some modern replica of the depression America went through in
the 1930s has now essentially vanished.

That awful, tragic event is referred to as the "Great Depression." Two features justify this description. One is its long
duration. The economy began descending into it in the summer
of 1929. Not until mid-1941, a dozen years later, was it over.
The second is its severity. For 1929, the average rate of unemployment was only 3.2 percent of the labor force, but then it
started growing. For 1931 it was 15.9 percent, and it exceeded
20.0 percent for each of the years 1932 through 1935. For 1933,
it peaked at 24.9 percent. That percentage translates into 12.8
million people unemployed in a labor force of 51.6 million.
From 1936 through 1940, the rate remained above 14.0 percent,
and even for 1941, it was 9.9 percent. By then, stimulus from
an unfortunate source—preparation for war—had begun to drive
it down.

Although this book and its companion on the New Deal
examine America's depression-related experiences, the depression
itself extended far beyond this one nation. For practical purposes,
it was worldwide. Among nations of economic significance, only
the Soviet Union managed to avoid it.

Once the depression was well under way, affected nations tried
to insulate themselves. America took the lead by passing the
Smoot-Hawley Tariff Act in 1930. It was an effort to "export
unemployment." Naturally, other nations followed suit. The
world's international trading system soon became a shambles.

The 1930s arrived on the heels of a decade with a very different spirit. It is often called the "Roaring Twenties" as a way
of suggesting its high spirits and general prosperity. Some of

what happened in the 1920s set the stage for the difficulties that followed.

In the middle of the 1920s, a speculative spirit took hold. It first manifested itself in a real estate boom in Florida. With property available for a down payment of ten percent and the promise of rapid appreciation, buyers surged in. However, in 1926, that speculative flurry collapsed.

In 1928, speculative energy zeroed in on a different arena: Wall Street. (Wall Street is literally a street in lower Manhattan where the New York Stock Exchange was, and still is, located, but it is also a symbolic name for an important segment of the nation's financial community.) That year's transactions on the New York Stock Exchange catapulted to 931 million shares, sixty percent above the 582 million traded in 1927 and more than double the 452 million traded in 1926. Purchases *on margin*—that is, largely on credit—were an important fuel for the booming market.

Once the boom ran out of steam, purchases on margin also helped propel the market's decline. When a speculator bought stock with borrowed money, the stock itself became collateral —security—for the loan. When the value of the stock declined, the speculator came under pressure either to put up more collateral or repay. Thus, when stock prices in general started going down rather than up, many speculators found themselves under mounting pressure to sell their holdings to raise the cash suddenly needed to repay loans.

The speculative fever lasted well into 1929. But then it ended. The market peaked in September, began declining, and ran into a rout towards the end of October. The rout, with prices tumbling, is what is meant by "the crash." Although general economic activity had begun its descent several months earlier, it is the stock market crash that is commonly thought of as the start of the era of the Great Depression. It is certainly an appropriate symbol of its beginning.

For the stock market, those losses late in October of 1929 turned out to be merely a sample of bad times still to come. From beginning to end, the market's decline lasted almost three years. When it was finally over in the summer of 1932, stocks were eighty-three percent below their peak in September of 1929. Once as high as $73, the price of a share of General Motors had fallen to $8, while for U.S. Steel, the decline had taken it from $262 to $22.

This unhappy story regarding Wall Street is only symptomatic of distress that erupted throughout the entire economy. During the three years following the crash, in the average week, around 100,000 people lost their jobs. In 1932, one million people in New York City were unemployed, while in Cleveland the unemployment rate was fifty percent, and in Toledo, eighty percent. Thousands of banks failed, and the protection that, since then, has come to be afforded to customers by federal deposit insurance did not yet exist. A few states actually defaulted, as did well over one thousand municipalities. From the top in 1929 to the bottom in 1933, the nation's total output fell over thirty percent. Not until 1937 did it regain its level in 1929, and then, in 1938, it took another sharp drop before resuming its growth.

Two men served as President during the depression. Herbert Hoover was elected in 1928 and assumed office in March of 1929. Soon thereafter the depression began, and it quickly threw his young presidency off stride. When he stood for reelection in 1932, the economy was in terrible shape, and Franklin D. Roosevelt won.

Through the years, Hoover's popular image has been somewhat unfairly tarnished over his handling of the depression. Hoover tried to deal with it and did have some productive approaches. Overall, however, he and others in his Administration were unaware that the forces at work were too powerful for the remedies they were willing to employ. By the time Roosevelt entered the presidency, he and the members of his Administration at least knew what kinds of efforts had been insufficient. It should be added that, of the two, Roosevelt was far the more effective in reassuring Americans that, with fortitude and ingenuity, the economic distress could be overcome.

In human terms, the effects of the depression were devastating and felt throughout the United States. People who had been solidly established found themselves adrift and unemployed. The rich obviously had a cushion of protection, but, at least in some ways, even they were affected. The wealthy financier J. P. Morgan, for example, decided to refrain from using his yacht for a time. "There are so many suffering from lack of work, and even actual hunger," he wrote to a friend in 1931, "that it is both wiser and kinder not to flaunt such luxuriant amusement in the face of the public."

As fall the leaves by Autumn blown,
So fell those lovely shares I own.
Forlorn, disconsolate I sing,
Goodbye, goodbye to everything!
To car and plane and gleaming yacht
And rather ducal country cot
That all seemed surely mine by Spring
Goodbye, goodbye to everything!
Farewell, farewell for evermore
To Paris, Carcassonne, Lahore
Day trips are all I now can swing.
Goodbye, goodbye to everything!

— L. H. Robbins,
The New York Times,
November 3, 1929

Around major cities, homeless, jobless people—sometimes entire families—drifted together into communities mockingly and bitterly referred to as "Hoovervilles." Their shelters were makeshift shacks, hovels pieced together with the likes of rusty auto bodies, tar paper, and other discarded materials.

People without jobs and fearing hunger made a receptive audience for labor unions. Unions capitalized upon long-standing currents of frustration to organize workers, increase their membership, and augment their influence. When industrialists tried to lower costs by reducing hours and wages, workers united to oppose them. Sometimes the conflict between workers and management escalated into violence. To cite one example, in Dearborn, Michigan on March 7, 1932, a Communist-instigated hunger march to the Ford Motor Company's River Rouge plant ended with four marchers dead and over sixty people injured.

Several months later, near the end of May, another era-defining confrontation began in and around Washington, D.C. A large contingent of World War I veterans began converging on the nation's capital. The group had initially been set in motion by a veteran named Walter W. Waters. Known as both the Bonus Army and the Bonus Expeditionary Force (BEF), they wanted to persuade Congress to allow them to receive promptly bonuses due them but not scheduled to be paid until 1945. Ravaged by the depression, the men had compelling needs for the money right then, not thirteen years later. Some camped out in tents. Many stayed in government buildings whose use President Hoover had approved. Estimates of the group's maximum membership range from fifteen to twenty thousand.

For some weeks the demonstration remained essentially amiable, and on June 15, the BEF got some encouragement when the House of Representatives passed a bill acceding to its wish. But two days later the Senate voted not to. Many veterans drifted away, but between eight and ten thousand stayed on. Over the following weeks, a few incidents broke out here and there, but mostly, the situation remained orderly. Then, towards the end of July, the Administration lost patience and decided that the veterans had to go. At first the assignment to move them out was thrust upon the police, but the situation soon escalated, and the Army was called in. The showdown was promptly a mismatch, made all the more so because General Douglas MacArthur, the Army's Chief of Staff, exceeded his orders. The protest was soon over, but the manner in which it ended spawned some radical, antiestablishment thoughts, even in the minds of people not often accustomed to entertaining them.

In 1930, American agriculture was a large sector; almost a quarter of the nation's population lived on farms. The depression brought individual farmers a range of experiences. While for many it was dreadful, in other instances, people living on farms fared acceptably because they at least had food and shelter. It is not surprising, therefore, that whereas the farm population had decreased by 1.4 million between 1920 and 1929, it grew by about one million between 1929 and 1933. Two important ingredients of this growth were a reduction in migration away from farms and an increase in the flow of people to them.

Although hard times were not universal among those living on farms during the depression, they were certainly widespread. Overall, the farming sector's income decreased dramatically. Net income (revenue minus cost) of farm operators and their employees fell from $7.0 billion in 1929 to $2.5 billion in 1932, a decline of sixty-four percent. As a result, many farmers were hard-pressed—and sometimes just unable—to pay taxes, mortgages, and other loans.

Farmers' financial stringency could lead to the use of force or the threat of it. Sometimes the aim would be to keep produce away from market in the hope of raising prices. At other times, it would be to intimidate would-be buyers at a foreclosure from bidding seriously so that friends or neighbors could purchase the property on the block for a pittance. In the fall of 1932, for example, one property near Haskens, Iowa, with an $800 mortgage, was purchased for $1.90. In this way farmers often got to remain on their property rather than being evicted.

While farms provided some with sanctuary, many others —including many African-Americans in the South—were not so fortunate. Many farm owners, sharecroppers, and tenants were driven from the land. Drought was an important factor. In that regard, the 1930s was a horrendous decade, and years of overgrazing and general inattention to conservation had made millions of acres especially vulnerable. The "Dust Bowl" developed over vast stretches of farmland in America's Great Plains from which wind would simply lift the parched, loose soil and carry it away.

Several million people were driven from the land. Typically they would go to a neighboring state, but many headed to the Far West, to Washington and Oregon and, in large numbers, to California. It was a displaced Oklahoma family's rugged pilgrimage to California that John Steinbeck so beautifully immortalized in *The Grapes of Wrath.*

Overall, farmers were feeling great strain. Speaking before a Senate committee, A. N. Young, president of the Farmers' Union of Wisconsin, communicated it:

> They are just ready to do anything to get even with the situation. I almost hate to express it, but I honestly believe that if some of them could buy airplanes they would come down here to Washington to blow you fellows all up....The farmer is naturally a conservative individual, but you cannot find a conservative farmer today....I am as conservative as any man could be, but any economic system that has in its power to set me and my wife in the streets, at my age—what can I see but red?

To provide some escape from misery in such grim times, even if only temporarily, Americans welcomed entertainment. They found it in such diversions as the movies, radio, sporting events, and parlor games. *Monopoly*, with its timely theme of rapidly changing economic fortunes—a player could be in financial euphoria one moment, disaster the next—struck an especially responsive chord. In 1935, Parker Brothers, which had recently acquired the game from its creator, Charles Darrow, was producing it at the rate of twenty thousand a week.

At best, however, entertainment and games could only provide intermittent diversion. The main theme of the period of the Great Depression is quite different. It is adversity. The era is a major landmark in American history because of the breadth, depth, and endurance of that adversity. It also happens to be a time of great significance in the history of economics as a discipline. During it, path-breaking progress was made towards understanding what causes depressions and, as a result, how to prevent them. The new knowledge started arriving too late to prevent the downturn that began in mid-1929 from escalating into the Great Depression, but it has certainly helped avoid a repetition. And, as selections following in this anthology well illustrate, that is a very good thing.

Economic Distress

Hoover's Early Warning

In this statement covering both foreign and domestic economics, then-Secretary of Commerce Herbert Hoover voices concerns regarding the inherent dangers of stock and real estate speculation.

Source: *The Commercial and Financial Chronicle*, January 2, 1926.

Any business forecast must be simply an appraisal of the forces in motion at home and abroad, for and against progress. All signs indicate that if we will temper our optimism with a sprinkling of caution we shall continue our high level of prosperity over 1926.

The United States has produced and consumed more goods in 1925 in proportion to population than ever before in its history. Our standard of living has therefore been the highest in our history and is of course the highest in the world. This improvement, however, has been greater in the urban centres than in agricultural communities.

The dominant favorable factor in our outlook is our increased productivity, due to fundamental and continuing forces—such as the cumulation of education, the advancement of science, skill and elimination of waste.

Other favorable indications on the immediate horizon are that the stocks of commodities are moderate; there is employment for practically everyone; real wages are at a high level; savings are the largest in history and capital is therefore abundant; and the whole machinery of production and distribution is operating at a higher degree of efficiency than ever before. While wholesale prices for the year as a whole have averaged about 6% higher than for the previous year it is largely due to needed advance in prices of agricultural products.

There are some phases of the situation which require caution. Continuation of real estate and stock speculation and its possible extension into commodities with inevitable inflation; the over-extension of installment buying; the extortion by foreign Government-fostered monopolies dominating our raw material imports; the continued economic instability of certain foreign countries; the lag in recovery of certain major agricultural products; the instability of the coal industry; the uncertainties of some important labor relationships—all these are matters of concern. But, as said above, with caution we should continue a prosperous year over 1926.

Agriculture, while it is better than it was two years ago, still leaves the farmers with much accumulated debt, and generally has not gained a stability that makes for contentment because its basic economic problem of market is unsolved. Also, it suffers from continued distortion in price relationship of the Middle West to the competing foreign countries because our transportation costs to seaboard have had to be increased more than those of its foreign competitors. The projected enlarged program of improvement in waterways is of great importance in this matter.

The construction industries have played a very large part in the high business activity of the past three years. The volume of construction has been unprecedented during the past year with consequent great activity in the construction-material industries, iron, steel, lumber, cement, etc. Contrary to normal expectations, this increased demand has not increased prices for there has been a slight reduction in building costs due in a large measure to the gradual lengthening of the building season. The increasing Federal, State and municipal public works programs for next year, together with the promise of large electrical and railway extension and improvement, indicate a continuing demand for heavy construction. While it might be thought that the war deficiency in housing has been overcome, yet the high real wage in industry creates a demand for better housing and this condition, combined with the migration to suburbs, due to the motor, promises to continue as long as employment remains general. We could hardly expect so exceptional a construction activity to repeat itself, but there will be a large volume in any event.

The textile and shoe industries as a whole are running at high levels of production, although the tendency in some branches of these industries to develop more rapidly in the South and West is affecting New England pending readjustment of her economic relationships. The automobile and tire industries will record an unprecedented output. The coal industries show increased production despite the anthracite strike and the production of all other minerals has increased.

In transportation, our railways are giving the best service in our history and are recovering in average earnings to near the Inter-State Commerce Commission standard of earnings of 5 3/4%. There is some improvement from the acute depression in the shipping world, and progress has been made in plans for internal waterway improvement. The electrification of the country has made further great strides during the year toward central generation and inter-connection. There has been some pyramiding of power holding companies, much criticized within the electrical industry itself, but the solid progress of the industry is marked by the extension of use of electricity with all its economies in production of goods and saving of labor. Furthermore, taking the country as a whole, there has been a reduction in rates for power and light, indicating that the public is securing benefits from the economies introduced in production of electricity.

Our foreign trade in 1925 has been exceptionally satisfactory. Both exports and imports have risen materially, the former reflecting an increase in agricultural exports and the latter reflecting the

large demand for foreign raw materials and tropical foodstuffs.
...The major explanation of our favorable trade balance is, of course, to be found in the continued heavy investment of American capital abroad; in essence we are lending foreigners the wherewithal to buy goods from us, or are sending goods to convey our investments abroad. It is probable that the final figures will show that this country has added to its foreign investments during the year by more than a billion dollars.

The most remarkable thing about the foreign trade of the United States is that, after making allowance for the higher level of prices, both exports and imports are much greater than before the war, in contrast with the quantitative decrease in the trade of the other foreign countries engaged in the war. According to British calculations, the exports of that country were in physical volume nearly 25% less in 1925 than before the war, and Germany's exports have fallen off still more. British imports are practically at their pre-war level, and those of Germany materially below it.

In finance, the year has been characterized by increased savings, comparatively easy money conditions, the issuance of a large volume of both domestic and foreign securities, and by an extraordinary rise in the prices of stocks, accompanied by marked speculation on the New York Stock Exchange. This fever of speculation is also widespread in real estate and unless our financial policies are guided with courage and wisdom, this speculation may yet reflect into the commodity markets, thereby reversing the cautious buying policies of recent years. Psychology plays a large part in business movements and over-optimism can only land us on the shores of over-depression. Not since 1920 have we required a better informed or more capable administration of credit facilities than now if we are to continue an uninterrupted high plane of prosperity. In any event there should be no abatement of caution in the placing of forward orders, particularly in view of the great increase in sales of a great variety of merchandise on the installment basis.

In the foreign field as a whole the situation is more promising than at any other time in 12 years. Each year one nation after another abroad gains in economic and fiscal stability, in production and in employment. War-inherited famines have disappeared from the earth, standards of living are everywhere higher than at any time since the war. In fact, no one in 1919 would have believed that so great a measure of recovery would be attained in Europe by 1925—a proof of a high quality in European statesmanship. The Locarno agreement promises much greater political stability, and paves the way for another stage of disarmament with consequent improvement in the economic outlook. Of the disturbed areas, England and Germany have not recovered employment in full; France shows economic strength among her people, but popular resistance has so far made it impossible to stabilize the fiscal system; China continues in the throes of civil war, but business, nevertheless, continues; Russia makes progress as the Government slowly abandons Socialism. The quantity of goods moving in international trade as a whole has recovered to the pre-war level, although some countries are below, and fully 90% of international business is now based upon stabilized currencies.

On the whole, both our own country and the rest of the world face a more favorable outlook at this turn of the year than for a long time past. We, ourselves, however, need to be on our guard against reckless optimism. What we need is an even keel in our financial controls, and our growing national efficiency will continue us in increasing prosperity.

Hoover Urges Banking Reform

In his memoirs, Hoover discussed weaknesses he had seen in the nation's banking system. For one thing, only one third of the banks belonged to the Federal Reserve System. In addition, many of the larger banks speculated in stocks, indirectly using —and losing—their depositors' money.

Source: Herbert Hoover, *Memoirs; The Great Depression,* Volume III (New York: The MacMillan Company, 1952).

A closed bank in Haverhill, Iowa. Photo by Rothstein

...[T]he American people had been living for some years under an illusion of the absolute security to be had from the Federal Reserve System. We were slow to realize the dangers in our banking system. These dangers were present in our inexpressibly feeble and badly organized deposit banking, credit and security promotion, structure, enhanced by lack of scruples among some leaders.

...I feel that our own banking and financial system was the worst part of the dismal tragedy with which I had to deal.

...Time and again from my first message to Congress, I urged the Congress to reform the banking laws to make depositors safe.

The public had become callous to bank failures because we had had over 4,000 such failures in the eight good years before the depression. More than 10,000 deposit institutions were to disappear in the five years after 1929, despite governmental props under the banking system....

Taking Action

In the following excerpts, Hoover recalls reactions to the October 1929 stock market crash.

Source: Herbert Hoover, *Memoirs; The Great Depression, Volume* III (New York: The MacMillan Company, 1952).

Two schools of thought quickly developed within our administration discussions.

First as the "leave it alone liquidationists" headed by Secretary of the Treasury [Andrew] Mellon, who felt that the government must keep its hands off and let the slump liquidate itself. Mr. Mellon had only one formula: "Liquidate labor, liquidate stocks, liquidate the farmers, liquidate real estate." ...He held that even a panic was not altogether a bad thing. He said: "It will purge the rottenness out of our system. High costs of living and high living will come down. People will work harder, live a more moral life. Values will be adjusted, and enterprising people will pick up the wrecks from less competent people."

But other members of the administration...believed with me that we should use the powers of government to cushion the situation....

... In the earlier stages we determined that the Federal government should use all of its powers:

(a) to avoid the bank depositors' and credit panics which had so generally accompanied previous violent slumps;

(b) to cushion slowly, by various devices, the inevitable liquidation of false values so as to prevent widespread bankruptcy and the losses of homes and productive power;

(c) to mitigate unemployment and to relieve those in actual distress;

(e) to prevent industrial conflict and social disorder;

(f) to preserve the financial strength of the United States government, our credit and our currency...in other words, to assure that America should meet every foreign debt, and keep the dollar ringing true on every counter in the world;

(g) to advance much-needed economic and social reforms as fast as could be...

(h) to sustain the morale and courage of the people in order that their initiative should remain unimpaired, and to secure from the people themselves every effort for their own salvation.

(i) to adhere rigidly to the Constitution and the fundamental liberties of the people.

"No One Has Starved"

Mellon pulled the whistle,
Hoover rang the bell,
Wall Street gave the signal
And the country went to Hell.

— Song of the Bonus Marchers, 1932

The September 1932 issue of Fortune *Magazine had a lengthy unsigned article challenging Hoover's assertion: "No one has starved." Fortune's study of the unemployment problem was one of the most detailed available for public reading at that time. The article appeared two months before the election that would replace Hoover in the White House by Roosevelt.*

...But the passage of the [Emergency Relief] Act...marks a turning in American political history. And the beginning of a new chapter in American unemployment relief. It constitutes an open and legible acknowledgment of governmental responsibility for the welfare of the victims of industrial unemployment. And its ultimate effect must be the substitution of an ordered, realistic, and intelligent relief program for the wasteful and uneconomic methods...employed during the first three years of the depression.

There can be no serious question of the failure of those methods. For the methods were never seriously capable of success....The theory was that private charitable organizations and semipublic welfare groups, established to care for the old and the sick and the indigent, were capable of caring for the casuals of a world-wide economic disaster. And the theory in application meant that social agencies manned for the service of a few hundred families, and city shelters set up to house and feed a handful of homeless men, were compelled by the brutal necessities of hunger to care for hundreds and thousands of families and whole armies of the displaced and the jobless. And to depend for their resources upon the contributions of communities no longer able to contribute, and upon the irresolution and vacillation of state legislatures and municipal assemblies long since in the red on their annual budgets....

But the psychological consequence was even worse. Since the problem was never frankly faced as facts, people came to believe that American unemployment was relatively unimportant. They saw little idleness and they therefore believed there was little idleness. It is possible to drive for blocks in the usual shopping and residential districts of New York and Chicago without seeing a breadline or a food station or a hungry mob or indeed anything else much more exciting than a few casuals asleep on a park bench. And for that reason, and because their newspapers played down the subject as an additional depressant in depressing times, and because they were bored with relief measures anyway, the great American public simply ignored the whole thing. They would still ignore it today were it not that the committee hearings and the Congressional debate and the Presidential veto of relief bills this last June attracted their attention. And that the final passage of the Emergency Relief and Construction Act of 1932 has committed their government and themselves to a policy of affirmative action which compels both it and them to know definitely and precisely what the existing situation is....

Having decided to at last face reality and do something about it, what is reality? How many men are unemployed in the U.S.? How many are in want? What are the facts?

The following minimal statements may be accepted as true —with the certainty that they underestimate that real situation:

1. Unemployment has steadily increased in the U.S. since the beginning of the depression and the rate of increase during the first part of 1932 was more rapid than in any other depression year.

2. The number of persons totally unemployed is now at least 10,000,000.

3. The number of persons totally unemployed next winter will, at the present rate of increase, be 11,000,000.

4. Eleven millions unemployed means better than one man out of every four employable workers.

5. This percentage is higher than the percentage of unemployed British workers registered under the compulsory insurance laws...higher than the French, the Italian, and the Canadian percentages, but lower than the German (43.9 per cent of trade unionists in April, 1932) and the Norwegian.

6. Eleven millions unemployed means 27,500,000 whose regular source of livelihood has been cut off.

7. Twenty-seven and a half millions without regular income includes the families of totally unemployed workers alone. Taking account of the numbers of workers on part time, the total of those without adequate income becomes 34,000,000 or better than a quarter of the entire population of the country.

8. Thirty-four million persons without adequate income does not mean 34,000,000 in present want. Many families have savings. But savings are eventually dissipated and the number in actual want tends to approximate the number without adequate income. ...it is conservative to estimate that the problem of next winter's relief is a problem of caring for approximately 25,000,000 souls. [These figures] are based upon estimates. For nothing but estimates exists. No heritage from the fumbling of the last three years is more discouraging than the complete lack of statistics. The Director of the President's Organization on Unemployment Relief, Mr. Walter S. Gifford...was forced to acknowledge before a subcommittee of the Senate in January, 1932, that he did not know, nor did his organization know, how many persons were out of work and in

need of assistance in the U.S. nor even how many persons were actually receiving aid at the time of his testimony....

But it is impossible to think or to act in units of 25,000,000 human beings....They are at once too large and too small. A handful of men and women and children digging for their rotten food in the St. Louis dumps are more numerous, humanly speaking, than all the millions that ever found themselves in an actuary's column. The 25,000,000 only become human in their cities and their mill towns and their mining villages. And their situation only becomes comprehensible in terms of the relief they have already received.

That is to say that the general situation can only be judged by the situation in the particular localities. But certain generalizations are possible. Of which the chief is the broad conclusion that few if any of the industrial areas have been able to maintain a minimum decency level of life for their unemployed. Budgetary standards as set up by welfare organizations, public and private, after years of experiment have been discarded. Food only, in most cases, is provided and little enough of that. Rents are seldom paid. Shoes and clothing are given in rare instances only. Money for doctors and dentists is not to be had. And free clinics are filled to overflowing. Weekly allowances per family have fallen as low as $2.39 in New York with $3 and $4 the rule in most cities and $5 a high figure.... "We are merely trying to prevent hunger and exposure," reported a St. Paul welfare head last may. And the same sentence would be echoed by workers in other cities with such additions as were reported at the same time from Pittsburgh where a cut of 50 per cent was regarded as "inevitable," from Dallas where Mexicans and Negroes were not given relief, from Alabama where discontinuance of relief in mining and agriculture was foreseen, from New Orleans where no new applicants were being received....

The Discovery of Poverty

In the introduction to her 1966 book The Invisible Scar, *Caroline Bird wrote "It is a curious fact that the Great Depression is in danger of disappearing altogether from the collective consciousness. Already it seems unreal, even to those who lived through it. Did those things really happen? We pinch ourselves. Wasn't it just a bad dream?" Here, Bird presents some of the faces of poverty.*

Source: Caroline Bird, *The Invisible Scar* (New York: Longman, Inc., 1966).

Shopfronts, Vicksburg, Mississippi, March, 1936, by Walker Evans. The South was hard hit by unemployment. Out-of-work farmers and factory workers hung up shingles to start their own businesses, but often there were no customers.

....

Everyone knew of someone engaged in a desperate struggle, although most of the agony went on behind closed doors. The stories were whispered. There was something indecent about

27

them. A well-to-do man living on the income from rental property could not collect his rents. His mortgages were foreclosed, and his houses sold for less than the debt. To make up the difference, he sold his own home. He moved himself and his wife into a nearby basement and did odd jobs for the people upstairs in exchange for a room for some of his six children. He mowed lawns, graded yards, and did whatever common labor he could find in order to pay for groceries, until his health broke down under the unaccustomed work. The doctor told him he needed an operation and would have to rest for a year afterward.

The New York Times *helped those among The Hundred Neediest Cases each year. By the standards of the rich at that time, these people were regarded as the "deserving poor," Bird explained, as distinguished from the "undeserving poor," who were thought to be unwilling to work or to save their money. The "deserving poor" were often the objects of charitable help from the rich. Unfortunately there were too many of them. Caroline Bird wrote:*

...A Brooklyn convent put sandwiches outside its door where the needy could get them without knocking. St. Louis society women distributed unsold food from restaurants. Someone put baskets in New York City railroad stations so that commuters could donate vegetables from their gardens....In San Francisco, the hotel and restaurant workers' union arranged for unemployed chefs and waiters to service elegant if simple meals to the unemployed....

...In New York City...there were enough hungry men without money to keep 82 badly managed breadlines going, and men were selling apples on every street corner....

No national charity existed to relieve mass poverty. The American Red Cross was big and efficient, but it had been set up to mobilize outside help for "a temporary condition brought about by some uncontrollable act or acts."...

A Quaker himself, Hoover went to the American Friends Service Committee. The Philadelphia Meeting developed a "concern" for the miners. Swarthmore and Haverford students ventured into the hollows, winning the confidence of suspicious miners. They systematically weighed the children so they could feed those in greatest need first. Hoover gave them $2,500 out of his own pocket, but most of the contributions seem to have come from the Rockefellers.

"No one has starved," Hoover boasted.

...People who were on public relief were denied civil rights. Some state constitutions disqualified relief clients from voting. ...In some places, village taxpayers' organizations tried to keep the children of tax delinquents out of the local schools. People suspected of taking public relief were even turned away from churches.

During the first and worst years of the Depression, the only public relief was improvised by cities. Appropriations were deliberately low. If funds ran out, so much the better. The poor would have to make another effort to find work....

State governments were not prepared to help. No state even had a Department of Welfare until Governor Franklin D. Roosevelt organized one for New York State in 1929. Cities begged for temporary loans, banks were generally reluctant because cities did not have tax resources from which to pay back the money....In January 1932, the New York City Department of Welfare did not have postage stamps on hand to distribute a million dollars raised and lent to the city by a committee of bankers.

Hoover kept insisting, no one starved....

Hooverville

Source: Charles R. Walker, "Relief and Revolution," *The Forum,* LXXXVIII (1932), pp. 73-74.

A few weeks ago I visited the incinerator and public dump at Youngstown, Ohio. Back of the garbage house there are at least three acres of waste land, humpy with ash heaps and junk. The area is not on the outskirts but in the middle of the steel mill district with furnaces near-by, and the tube mills and factory stacks of Youngstown. The dump is a kind of valley with a railroad embankment flanking it. As you approach from the garbage house, certain excrescences compete in vision with the ash humps and junk. They appear more organized than the rest of the place, but one is not sure. When, however, you come close, there is no doubt but the dump is inhabited.

The place is indeed a shanty town, or rather a collection of shanty hamlets, for the separate blotches are not all in one place but break out at intervals from the dump. Some of them are caves with tin roofs, but all of them blend with the place, for they are constructed out of it. From 150 to 200 men live in shanties. The place is called by its inhabitants—Hooverville.

I went forward and talked to the men; they showed me their houses. These vary greatly from mere caves covered with a piece of tin, to weather-proof shanties built of packing boxes and equipped with a stolen window-frame or an improved door. Some have beds and one or two a kitchen stove rescued from the junk heap, though most of the men cook in communal fashion over a fire shielded by bricks in the open.

The inhabitants were not, as one might expect, outcasts or "untouchables," or even hoboes in the American sense; they were men without jobs. Life is sustained by begging, eating at the city soup kitchens, or earning a quarter by polishing an automobile—enough to bring home bacon and bread. Eating "at home" is preferred. The location of the town also has its commissary advantage; men take part of their food from the garbage house. This I entered; the stench of decaying food is appalling. Here I found that there were more women than men—gathering food for their families. In Hooverville there are no women.

This pitiable village would be of little significance if it existed only in Youngstown, but nearly every town in the United States has it shanty town for the unemployed, and the same instinct has named them all "Hooverville." The Pittsburgh unit has been taken under the wing of Father Cox—of Hunger March fame—who feeds the inhabitants at a soup kitchen in the cellar of his church, and who has supplied each shanty with a printed postcard: "God Bless Our Home." The largest Hooverville in the United States is in St. Louis, with a hovel population of 1200. Chicago had a flourishing one, but it was felt to be an affront to municipal pride and was ordered burned. The inhabitants were summarily told to get out, and thirty minutes later the "homes" were in ashes.

In the Hooverville of Ambridge, Pennsylvania, I met a man with whom I talked a long time. He was a Slav who had come to this country thirty years ago, and who had grown sons somewhere, though he had lost touch with them. As a veteran worker, he reminisced over many jobs, skilled and unskilled, in the American mills. But he had now lost his last one. Standing in front of the huts and clasping the fist of one hand with the other, he said to me, "If you had told me, when I come to this country that now I live here like dis, I shot you dead."

Southern Negroes Felt the Depression Later

Celebrated author and poet Maya Angelou described her child-hood in Stamps, Kansas in her autobiography. Following are two excerpts from that book.

Source: *I Know Why the Caged Bird Sings,* copyright Maya Angelou, 1969. Reprinted by permission of Random House, Inc., pp. 41-42.

....

During the summer we went barefoot, except on Sunday, and we learned to resole our shoes when they "gave out," as Momma used to say. The Depression must have hit the white section of Stamps with cyclonic impact, but it seeped into the Black area slowly, like a thief with misgivings. The country had been in the throes of the Depression for two years before the Negroes in Stamps knew it. I think that everyone thought that the Depression, like everything else, was for the whitefolks, so it had nothing to do with them. Our people had lived off the land and counted on cotton-picking and hoeing and chopping seasons to bring in the cash needed to buy shoes, clothes, books and light farm equipment. It was when the owners of cotton fields dropped the payment of ten cents for a pound of cotton to eight, seven and finally five that the Negro community realized that the Depression, at least, did not discriminate.

Welfare agencies gave food to the poor families, Black and white. Gallons of lard, flour, salt, powdered eggs and powdered milk. People stopped trying to raise hogs because it was too difficult to get slop rich enough to feed them, and no one had the money to buy mash or fish meal.

Momma spent many nights figuring on our tablets, slowly. She was trying to find a way to keep her business going, although her customers had no money. When she came to her conclusions, she said, "Bailey, I want you to make me a nice clear sign. Nice and neat. And Sister, you can color it with your Crayolas. I want it to say:

1 5 LB. CAN OF POWDERED MILK IS WORTH 50¢ IN TRADE
1 5 LB. CAN OF POWDERED EGGS IS WORTH $1.00 IN TRADE
10 #2 CANS OF MACKEREL IS WORTH $1.00 IN TRADE."

And so on. Momma kept her store going. ...

In March 1932, as the Great Depression continued, people were forced to beg for food. Some met in soup kitchens and bread-lines (community centers set up to distribute soup to hungry people) and Hoovervilles. Songs and poems grew out of this despair. The author of the following song is not known.

Beans, Bacon, and Gravy

I was born long ago
In eighteen ninety-one
And I've seen many a panic, I will own.
I've been hungry, I've been cold,
And now I'm growing old,
But the worst I've seen is nineteen thirty-one.

Chorus:

Oh, those beans, bacon, and gravy,
They almost drive me crazy!
I eat them till I see them in my dreams.
When I wake up in the morning
And another day is dawning,
Then I know I'll have another mess of beans.

We all congregate each morning
At the county barn at dawning,
And everyone is happy, so it seems.
But when our work is done
We file in one by one
And thank the Lord for one more mess of beans.

We have Hooverized on butter,
And for milk we've only water,
And I haven't seen a steak in many a day
As for pies, cakes, and jellies,
We substitute sow-bellies
For which we work the county road each day.

If there ever comes a time
When I have more than a dime,
They will have to put me under lock and key,
For they've had me broke so long
I can only sing this song
Of the workers and their misery.

The Bonus Expeditionary Force

In 1924, Congress agreed to pay World War I veterans a
bonus of $1 a day for each day of service in the U.S.; $1.25 per
day for each day of service overseas. The bonus was to be paid
in 1945. During the Great Depression the demand grew for im-
mediate payment of the bonus, and many veterans or members
of their families wrote emotional letters to Hoover's President's
Committee for Unemployment Relief. Some of those letters
follow. Note: The letters are reprinted as the people wrote them,
including any spelling or grammatical errors.

Source: Robert McElvaine, *Down and Out in the Great Depression: Letters
from the Forgotten Man* (Chapel Hill, North Carolina: University of North
Carolina Press, 1983).

Oil City, Penna.
December 15, 1930

Col. Arthur Woods
Director, Presidents Committee*

Dear Sir:

...Now that our income is but $15.60 a week (their are five
of us My husband Three little children and myself). My husband
who is a world war Veteran and saw active service in the trenches,
became desperate and applied for Compensation or a pension
from the Government and was turned down and that started me
thinking....[There] should be enough to pay all world war veterans a pension, dysabeled or not dysabeled and there by relieve a
lot of suffering, and banish resentment that causes Rebellions
and Bolshevism. Oh why is it that it is allways a bunch of
overely rich, selfish, dumb, ignorant money hogs that persist
in being Senitors, legislatures, representatives Where would they
and their possessions be if it were not for the Common Soldier,
the common laborer that is compelled to work for a starvation

34

wage. for I tell you again the hog of a Landlord gets his there is not enough left for the necessaries if a man has three or more children....

Very Truly Yours

Mrs. M.E.B.

* Director of Hoover's President Committee for Unemployment Relief.

Detroit, Michigan

September 29, 1931

Mr. Walter Gifford,*

You have told us to spend to end the slump, but you did not tell us what to use for money, after being out of work for two years you tell us this. Pres. Hoover on the one hand tells the working man to build homes, and in the face of the fact nearly every working man has had his home taken off him... Mr. Gifford why not come clean, and stop bluffing us. Tell us the reason of the depression is greed of Bankers and Industrialists who are taking too great of amount of profits....The other day our Pres. Hoover came to Detroit and kidded the soldier boys out of their bonus. Pres. Hoover a millionaire worth about 12,000,000 dollars drawing a salary of 75,000 dollars per year from the government asking some boys to forgo their bonus some of them have not 12 dollars of their own....

J.B.

*Walter Gifford replaced Arthur Woods as head of President's Organization for Unemployment Relief.

Letters from the Forgotten Man

Robert McElvaine believed that the best way to know the people at the time of the Depression was to read what they had to say. Approximately 15,000 letters were examined to prepare his book Down and Out in the Great Depression: Letters from the Forgotten Man *(Chapel Hill, North Carolina: University of North Carolina Press, 1983). Some excerpts help us understand the despair. The title comes from Roosevelt's promise to help the forgotten man at the bottom of the economic pyramid.*

For the first three years of the Great Depression, the letters were sent to President Hoover and the people in charge of his programs. They were primarily from well-to-do citizens. They show the attitudes of those who believed that people could survive and get jobs if they just tried harder, as in the letter of W.H.H.

In the weeks following Franklin Roosevelt's inauguration, 450,000 letters poured into the White House. For years, the average remained at 5000 to 8000 per day. Many were addressed to Eleanor Roosevelt, the President's wife. People believed that she would serve as an intermediary between them and the President. These letters were generally answered promptly and, if possible, signed by the President. Some fifteen million of the letters are preserved at the Franklin D. Roosevelt Library in Hyde Park, New York; others are in the National Archives.

These letters are reprinted as the people wrote them.

Annapolis, Maryland
September 10, 1931

My Dear Mr. Hoover,

It is my purpose to write you a short letter and to cheer you along with your trying undertakings....

In these days of unrest and general dissatisfaction it is absolutely impossible for a man in your position to get a clear and impartial view of the general conditions of things in America today. But, of this fact I am very certain, that there is not five per cent of the poverty, distress and general unemployment that many of your enemies would have us believe. It is true, that there is much unrest, but this unrest is largely caused—by the excessive prosperity and general debauchery through which the country has traveled since the period of the war. The result being that in three cases out of four, the unemployed is looking for a very light job at a very heavy pay, and with the privilege of being provided with an automobile if he is required to walk more than four or five blocks a day....

Sincerely,
[W.H.H.]

Goff Kansas
May 10, 1935

Mrs. Franklin D. Roosevelt:
My Dear Friend:

For the first time of my lifetime I am asking a favor and this one I am needing very badly and I am coming to you for help.

Among your friends do you know of one who is discarding a spring coat for a new one. If so could you beg the old one for me. I wear a size 40 to 42 I have not had a spring coat for six years and last Sunday when getting ready to go to church I see my winter coat had several very thin places in the back that is very noticeable My clothes are very plain so I could wear only something plain. we were hit very hard by the drought and every penny we can save goes for feed to put in crop.

Hoping for a favorable reply.

Your friend Mrs. J.T.

Mr. and Mrs. Roosevelt
Wash. D.C.
February 1936

Dear Mr. President,

I am a boy of 12 years. I want to tell you about my family.
My father hasn't worked for 5 months. He went plenty times
to relief, he filed out application. They won't give us anything.
I don't know why. Please you do something. We haven't paid
4 months rent, Everyday the landlord rings the bell, we don't
open the door for him. We are afraid that will be put out, been
put out before, and don't want to happen again. We haven't paid
the gas bill, and the electric bill, haven't paid grocery bill for 3
months. My bother goes to Lane Tech. High School. he's
eighteen years old, hasn't gone to school for 2 weeks because
he got no carfare. I have a sister she's twenty years, she can't
find work. My father he staying home. All the time he's crying
because he can't find work. i told him why are you crying daddy,
and daddy said why shouldn't I cry when there is nothing in the
house. I feel sorry for him. That night I couldn't sleep. The
next morning I wrote this letter to you. in my room. Were
American citizens and were born in Chicago, Ill. and I don't
know why they don't help us Please answer right away because
we need it. Will starve Thank you
　God bless you

　　　　　　　　　　　　　　　　[Anonymous]
　　　　　　　　　　　　　　　　Chicago, Ill.

Entertainment to Lighten the Heart

Who's Afraid of the Big Bad Wolf?

by
Janet Beyer

During the Great Depression, people desperately needed to
be given a break, however brief, from their daily concerns.
The motion picture industry provided such relief. Lighthearted
movies presented child star Shirley Temple, who, in her films,
conquered adversity and poverty to live happily forever after. The
musical extravaganzas of Busby Berkley featured line after line of
elegantly costumed dancers in lavish settings. And the gorgeous
Fred Astaire and Ginger Rogers danced and smiled their way into
everyone's heart.

The reality of the hard times were also reflected in the movies
and in the songs of the thirties. Gangster movies, in which "the
bad" poor guys took on "the rich," were prevalent. Although the
gangsters were punished at the end of the film, there was a certain
sympathy for them and their plight. Even animated films reflected
the distress of the times. Betty Boop, a popular cartoon sweet-
heart, was shown losing her farm to the bank in one episode.

"Who's Afraid of the Big Bad Wolf" was sung by the three
little pigs in the Walt Disney cartoon, and may be the most typi-
cal of popular depression songs. The Big Bad Wolf represented
the Great Depression, and the people (the little pigs) were determined not to be afraid.

Variety Magazine recorded the top musical hits of the day, and
the songs reflected both the despair of the Depression and the need
to escape.

People found free entertainment at home by listening to the
radio. Bing Crosby, Rudy Vallee, Maurice Chevalier, Gene
Autry, and the Boswell Sisters were popular.

"Brother Can you Spare a Dime?" *was popularized by Bing Crosby.*

Source: E.V. "Yip" Harburg, 1928; Copyright 1932 by Harms, Inc

---

Brother, Can You Spare A Dime?

They used to tell me I was building a dream—,
And so I followed the mob—
When there was earth to plough or guns to bear
I was always there, right on the job.
They used to tell me I was building a dream
With peace and glory ahead—
Why should I be standing in line
Just waiting for bread?
Refrain:
Once I built a railroad,
Made it run on time.
Once I built a railroad,
Now it's done—
Brother, can you spare a dime?
Once I built a tower, to the sun.
Brick and rivet and lime,
Once I built a tower
Now it's done—
Brother, can you spare a dime?
Once in khaki suits,
Gee, we looked swell,
Full of the Yankee Doodle-de-dum.
Half a million boots went sloggin' thru Hell,
I was the kid with the drum.
Say don't you remember, they called me Al—
It was Al all the time.
Say, don't you remember I'm your pal—
Buddy, can you spare a dime?

Ideal Women

Shirley Temple was the most amazing film phenomenon.
The talented curly-haired youngster was the number-one box
office-office attraction between 1935 and 1938. By 1940, she
had starred in twenty-one films. There were Shirley Temple
dolls, books, spoons, and dishes. Seeing a way out of poverty,
mothers taught their daughters to tap dance. Young girls' hair,
grown into ringlets that framed the face, were the rage. For the
mothers, Katharine Hepburn, Claudette Colbert, and Rosalind
Russell were most admired as fast-talking, witty, talented, pro-
fessional women. Susan Ware describes some of the celebrities
who helped many cope with the Great Depression years.

Source: Susan Ware, *Holding Their Own, American Women in the 1930s*
(Boston, MA: Twayne Publishers, 1982).

"During the 1930s, Eleanor Roosevelt, Sonja Henie [figure
skater], Babe Didrickson [golfer and all-round athlete], and Amelia
Earhart [airplane pilot], shared the limelight with colorful figures
from the world of entertainment. It was the era of hot jazz im-
provisation called swing music, and the country delighted in the
singing of Bessie Smith....and Ethel Waters....But the real stars
of the 1930s were movie actresses, the new cultural standard-
bearers of twentieth-century America. Movie stars had replaced
figures in politics, business, and the arts as the most popular role
models for American youth.

The movies dominated American popular culture from the
1920s through the 1940s but they played an especially large role
during the 1930s. Movies provided diversion and escape from the
grim economic news coming over the radio or in the daily newspaper; screwball comedies and Busby Berkeley extravaganzas took
the public's mind off the Depression. Movies also reinforced
traditional American mores and played an important role in prop-
ping up the collective spirit of the country during the hardship

of the 1930s. Unlike other forms of entertainment, movies kept their audiences during the Depression; between 60 and 90 million Americans attended movies each week during the 1930s. For many families the 10 cent for a weekly movie was as important an item in their budget as bread or milk."

A Super Hero

Superman's first appearance

Comic books, or comic magazines as they were called then, were born during the thirties and many of these featured super heroes. The first and most popular of these was Superman. He represented an ordinary person who could win against all odds. He could overcome any adversity, and the people of the Depression needed to know that was possible. The first issue in which Detective Comics put Superman on the cover was published in June 1938. With his almost unlimited powers, X-ray vision, ability to leap tall buildings in a single bound, the Man of Steel became a favorite of the people who had seen themselves for too long as being powerless.

The Women Get Involved

"Pocketbook Patriotism"

During the early 1930s, the Ladies Home Journal *was filled with household hints, party ideas, fashions from France, interviews with famous women, romantic stories and a sub-deb section, instructing young women how to improve posture, etiquette, personality, and appearance. There was only a hint of the widespread hardship. The editorial page, however, did tackle the issue with some suggestions on combating the shattered economy.*

In February 1932, an unsigned editorial called for "Pocketbook Patriotism."

The pocketbook of the American woman is the barometer of American business. In boom times she is a liberal spender. In bad times she is a desperate hoarder of money. Right now, if she opens her purse, she can help end the depression. For more than two years the whole nation has been seeking a program for prosperity. Hundreds of panaceas have been put forward. Millions and billions of dollars have been called for. Great machines of government and finance have been set up.

But only fear fed on these plans. Food supplies have been cut down. Old clothes have been stylish. Homes have fallen into disrepair. Ancient motor cars have been driven. Old equipment has not been replaced. Cash has been in hiding and not at work.

The women can help stop the depression right now. They can make money doing it too.

A billion and a half frightened dollars have been hoarded. Idle money, which makes idle men.

Samuel Crowther, in a subsequent editorial (March 1932) in the Ladies Home Journal, *challenged women:*

...If you do not exercise [your] purchasing power—that is, if you do not buy in your usual and reasonable fashion—you are cheating yourself of bargains and also in the end—you will cheat yourself of your income.

For, if no one buys beyond the bare necessities, the volume of business will go still lower and your income, no matter how solidly it seems to be founded, will come down in the chaos brought about by destructive thrift.

Cast a balance sheet on your own finances and see if you are financially hard up or only mentally hard up.

Women frequently found themselves less disrupted by the depression than men. Men lost their jobs and had difficulty finding new ones, but women were used to being at home and had made a life of making do with whatever they had available. Although women had less money to spend, prices had dropped significantly, helping them to compensate for the reduction in family income.

Source: Susan Ware, *Holding Their Own: American Women in the Depression* (Boston, MA: Twayne Publishers, 1982).

With some creative shopping and cooking, a woman could feed a family of six on $5 a week, with milk at 10 cents a quart, a loaf of bread 7 cents, butter 23 cents a pound, and two pounds of hamburger for 25 cents. ...

Women shared inexpensive recipes:

Green Tomato Mincemeat

1 pk green tomatoes	2 t cinnamon
1/2 pk apples	1/2 t cloves
1/2 cup butter	1 box raisins
5 c white sugar	1 c cider vinegar

Grind tomatoes and apples, mix other ingredients, and cook for two hours. Place in nine-inch pie shells and bake 375°. Makes six or seven pies.

The Women's Emergency Brigade
at Flint, Michigan

by
Janet Beyer

The unemployment of the depression added to continuing
unfair labor practices, despite legislation to end such practices,
and brought to a head the unrest among workers that had been
brewing for several decades. Union organizers were able to make
considerable progress, perhaps because the workers had so little
to lose. Many employers, seeing in the depression the oppor-
tunity for lower wages and longer hours, fought the unions.
One reason the automobile industry was particularly hurt by the
depression was because people did not have money to buy cars.

In January 1937, the workers at the General Motors' Chevrolet
plant in Flint, Michigan sat down on the job and would not
leave the plant. This was one of the first "sit-down strikes" in
the country. A committee chaired by Senator Robert La Follette
had found General Motors guilty of corporate espionage and
union-busting activities, in violation of New Deal legislation.
This strike was one of the most crucial of the decade, and ended
in victory for the workers.

On January 11, in below zero-weather, the company turned
off the heat in one building. Strike supporters were forbidden
to deliver food to the men. A battle waged between police and
workers for three hours, ending in victory for the United Auto
Workers. The new governor, Frank Murphy, sent in the
National Guard but, sympathetic to the workers, refused to
have them break the strike.

Three days later, twenty-three-year-old Genora Johnson organized the Women's Emergency Brigade. It was made up of women
who were willing to stand between the strikers and any force that
would try to break the strike.

45

The strike, which spread to other GM buildings, lasted about six weeks. During the month the women had to march from one building to another to protect strikers in other sections of the plant. Women gathered from other cities to fortify the march.

Mary Heaton Vorse wrote about the Flint strike. She was a journalist and labor activist.

Source: Dee Garrison, ed., *Rebel Pen, the Writings of Mary Heaton Vorse* (New York: Monthly Review Press, 1985). First printed in *Eye Opener* by Mary Heaton Vorse, 1937.

The hall downstairs was full of red-capped women with EB (Emergency Brigade) on their arms. There was a large contingent of women with green tams and green armbands. They were members of the Detroit Women's Auxiliary, before whom members of the Flint EB spoke in Detroit. Already a thriving brigade is being organized that will wear blue tams. Brigades are springing up wherever cars are being made.

"Before we are through, there will be Emergency Brigades in steel, in rubber—wherever there are women's auxiliaries," a woman said.

Five hundred women are making history, since there is the first EB parade that has even been held. The march around the business district was only the beginning. Soon the women were in cars on their way to the picket line around Fisher One.

Here they take part in one of the most amazing demonstrations this country has ever seen. Veterans in the labor movement insisted they had never seen anything like it. Six deep the pickets marched around and around the factory. The picket line enfolded the great plant. Thousands of people on the picket line. Thousands of strike sympathizers looking on. Thousands of singing men and women guarding the sitdown strikers from the threat of violent eviction after the injunction has been granted.

Ten thousand people in all must have assembled here, and a note of color was added by the hundreds of bright red and green hats. Not a policeman was in sight. The traffic was patrolled by the strikers themselves. Late in the afternoon the central strike committee at the request of the sheriff sent word to the crowd without disorder. Not one unfortunate incident marred the afternoon. The immense crowd was handled by the workers themselves. It is an example of how workers manage things when police do not interfere.

After dinner at the union kitchen the women adjourned to the meeting in Pengelly Hall.

What a meeting!

The hall was already packed by half past six, although the meeting was scheduled for eight and remained crowded until long after midnight. The women ran their own meeting, and the most significant speeches were made by women from various towns, because here you saw a real women's movement in the making. Saw it forming before your eyes. Something creative and vital, stirring through the working women of the country.

A woman from Detroit gets up "Our auxiliary is growing by leaps and bounds," she said. "We are expanding in all sorts of ways. The children come in from five to six in the evening for singing. We put on amateur shows about strike incidents...."

Another woman speaks: "I'm not a very good speaker, but I'm a very good sitter. I sat twenty-four days in the Bohn Aluminum plant. Since we won our strike things have gone fine."

The home and the union are becoming fused. In several places the women are starting nurseries in the union hall. The young girls cooperate in taking care of the babies. A new era is coming to the women in the automobile industry.

Dorothy Day and the Bread Lines

Dorothy Day spent her life taking care of people in need; she chose to live in poverty in the Lower East Side of New York, which was the headquarters for a newspaper she published, The Catholic Worker. *During the Depression she became very active and ran Hospitality Houses in New York for the homeless.*

Following is an interview by Studs Terkel from his book on the Depression.

Source: Studs Terkel, *Hard Times* (Pantheon Books, New York: 1970).

...We didn't intend to have a bread line or a soup line come to the door. During the Seamen's Strike of 1937, six of them showed up....We took in about ten seamen. We rented a store-front, while the strike lasted for three months. We had big tubs of cottage cheese and peanut butter, and bread by the ton brought in. They could make sandwiches all day and there was coffee on the stove.

While we were doing that for the seamen, one of the fellows on the Bowery [a section of New York noted for having many poor and homeless people] said, "What...are you doing down there feeding the seamen? What about the people on the Bowery? Nobody's feeding them." ...That's how the first bread line started. Pretty soon we had a thousand men coming in a day, during the Depression. It started simply because that Bowery guy got mad.

The Face of the People

Post Office, Nethers, Virginia, October 1935. Photo by Rothstein

Farm Life

In the Tennessee Valley, overproduction and poor farm management caused an erosion of soil. The soil washed into the Mississippi River and the Gulf of Mexico. Overproduction of cotton crops in the south caused the price of cotton to drop to a point where it was not worth selling.

Without money people were not buying.

Tenant farmers, sharecroppers, and migrant farmers were the most severely affected. There was nothing to farm and no money for wages. They were not able to pay their rent, produce crops, or find work.

Writer James Agee and photographer Walker Evans were commissioned by Fortune *magazine to document the daily life of tenant farmers and sharecroppers in the Deep South. They lived with three families in Alabama for about six weeks, sharing the families' food and sleeping in their houses. Their work was rejected by the magazine and was published in 1941 as* "Let Us Now Praise Famous Men." *It has become a classic depression-era book. The families are the Woods, the Gudgers and the Rickets. They harvest corn and cotton. The excerpts below are from Agee's essays.*

Source: James Agee and Walker Evans, *Let us Now Praise Famous Men* (Ballantine Walden Books, New York: 1966).

....

Gudger is a straight half-cropper, or sharecropper.

Woods and Rickets own no home and no land, but Woods owns one mule and Rickets owns two, and they own their farming implements. Since they do not have to rent these tools and animals, they work under a slightly different arrangement. They give over to the landlord only a third of their cotton and a fourth of their corn. Out of their own parts of the crop, however, they owe him the price of two thirds of their cotton fertilizer and three fourths of their corn fertilizer, plus interest; and, plus interest, the same debts or rations money.

Woods and Rickets are tenants....

A very few tenants pay cash rent: but these two types of arrangement, with local variants (company stores; food instead of rations money; slightly different division of the crops) are basic to cotton tenantry all over the South.

....

Gudger—a family of six—lives on ten dollars a month rations during four months of the year. He has lived on eight, and on six. Woods—a family of six—until this year was unable to get better than eight a month during the same period; this year he managed to get it up to ten. Rickets—a family of nine—lives on ten dollars a month during this spring and early summer period.

This debt is paid back in the fall at eight per cent interest. Eight per cent is charged also on the fertilizer and on all other debts which tenants incur in this vicinity.

Working on third and fourth, a tenant gets the money from two thirds of the cottonseed of each bale: nine dollars to the bale. Woods, with a mule, makes three bales, and gets twenty-seven dollars. Rickets, with two mules, makes and gets twice that, to live on during the late summer....

Cider stand, Blue Ridge Mountains, VA, 1935. Photo by Rothstein

It is not often, then, at the end of the season, that a tenant clears enough money to tide him through the winter, or even an appreciable part of it. ...

The Beds

The children's bed in the rear room has a worn-out and rusted mesh spring; the springs of the two beds are wire net, likewise rusty and exhausted. Aside from this and from details formerly mentioned, the beds many be described as one. There are two mattresses on each, both very thin, padded, I would judge, one with raw cotton and one with cornshucks. They smell old, stale and moist and are morbid with bedbugs, with fleas, and, I believe, with lice. They are homemade. The sheaths are not ticking, but rather weak unbleached cotton. Though the padding is sewn through, to secure it, it has become uncomfortably lumpy in some places, nothing but cloth in others. ...The mattresses and springs are loud, each in a different way, to any motion. The springs sag so deeply that two or more, sleeping here, fall together at the middle almost as in a hammock. ...

Clothing

Louise: The dress she wore most was sewn into one piece of two materials, an upper half of faded yellow-checked gingham, and a skirt made of a half-transparent flour sack, and beneath this, the bulk of a pinned, I presume flour sack clout; and a gingham bow at the small of the back, and trimming at the neck. She has two other dresses, which are worn to Cookstown or for sundays, and are, I imagine, being saved for school. They too are made painstakingly to be pretty, and as much as possible like pattern and ready-made dresses. During the week she is always bare-footed and wears a wide straw hat in the sun. Her mother dresses her carefully in the idiom of a little girl a year or two littler than she is. On sundays she wears slippers and socks, and a narrow blue ribbon in her hair, and a many times laundered white cloth hat.

Junior: ready-made overalls, one pair old, one not far from new, the newer cuffs turned up; a straw hat; bare feet, which are one crust of dew-poised sores; a ready-made blue shirt; a homemade gray shirt; a small straw hat. On sunday, clean overalls, a white shirt, a dark frayed necktie, a small, frayed, clean gray cap.

Burt: Two changes of cloths. One is overalls and one of two shirts, the other is a suit. The overalls are homemade out of pale tan cotton. One of the shirts is pale blue, the other is white; they are made apparently of pillowslip cotton. The collars are flared open: "sport collars," and the sleeves end nearer the shoulder than the elbow. The suit, which is old and, though carefully kept, much faded, is either a ready-made extravaganza or a hard-worked imitation of one. It is sewn together, pants and an upper piece, the pants pale blue, the upper piece white, with a small rabbit-like collar. There are six large white non-functional buttons sewn against the blue at the waistline....

Interior of Ozark cabin, Missouri, May 1936. Photo by Mydans

Katy and Flora Merry Lee are of the same size and use each other's clothes. They have between them perhaps three dresses made of the sheeting, with short sleeves and widened skirts, and shirts or blouses made of thin washed flour sacking, and each has a pair of sheeting overalls. ...They have no "sunday" clothes; for Sunday they wear the least unclean of these dresses, and a few cheap pins, necklaces and lockets. During the week as well as on Sunday they sometimes tie dirty blue ribbons into their hair, and sometimes shoestrings.

And If You Were Sick...

In 1932, Dr. Lewis Andreas was a founding member of Chicago's first medial center—a group practice with low fees. Writer Studs Terkel recorded this interview with Dr. Andreas.

Source: Studs Terkel, *Hard Times* (Pantheon Books, New York: 1970).

The poor people would not hesitate to go to free clinics, there was no loss of self-respect for them. They were used to this business. But the middle class couldn't drag itself to that point.

People fairly well-off suddenly found themselves without funds....We had a lot of teachers among our patients.

They couldn't afford to get medical care and they couldn't bring themselves to sitting in a dispensary. They put off care until things got real bad. They probably lost their lives.

The spirit of the free hospital and the spirit of the free clinic was the spirit of the alms house....

All of a sudden I find myself taking care of an ex-president of a university. And there was a widow of the curator of an art museum, well dressed, white hair, genteel....it was a mixture of people, with one common denominator: difficulty in paying their medical bills.

And people starved on the street and on streetcars. Every day ...somebody would faint on a streetcar. They'd bring him in, and

54

they wouldn't ask any questions. They'd look the patient over briefly. The picture was familiar. They knew what it was. Hunger. When he regained consciousness, they'd give him something to eat....

Thinking back, he told Terkel:

My habit of life has been changed by the Depression. ...the wounds are permanent. My father was a doctor, and his life savings were in one piece of property. It was foreclosed on him....and he lost every cent he had. They simply took it away because they had the legal right to take it away....So there was no help from Papa anymore. I had planned research work, but the Depression got me into this—I don't have too many regrets. I would have been a nice rich guy, probably, with a practice. ...As it is , I'm myself, unique....I have no regrets.

The Dust Bowl

The farmers of the midwest were hit particularly hard during the depression. The fertile topsoil they depended on for good crops had been lost during a three-year drought. Because money was scarce, the bankers who held the mortgages on the farms began demanding their payment. The farmers had none and were forced to leave their homes. Even farm families who owned their land were unable to farm because of the poor condition of the soil.

Poor soil was not a problem in California. Many farm families loaded their belongings in their trucks and headed west. They did not have the money to buy land, but hoped to be able to find jobs on farms in the fertile valleys of California.

John Steinbeck was a native of the Monterey peninsula in central California. Many migrant farm families came to that area. The Grapes of Wrath, *his book about an Oklahoma migrant family, the Joads, described the desperate, but hopeful life of these people. The first chapter of the book details the severity of the drought and dust storms that invaded Oklahoma.*

Source: John Steinbeck, *The Grapes of Wrath* (First printed in 1939, reissued by Viking Press, 1959).

...In the last part of May the sky grew pale and the clouds that had hung in high puffs for so long in the spring were dissipated. The sun flared down on the growing corn day after day until a line of brown spread along the edge of each green bayonet. The clouds appeared, and went away, and in a while they did not try any more. The weeds grew darker green to protect themselves, and they did not spread any more. The surface of the earth crusted, a thin hard crust, and as the sky became pale, so the earth became pale, pink in the red country and white in the gray country.

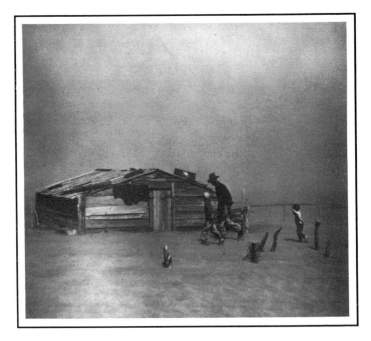

Farmer and his sons walking through a dust storm, Cimarron County, Oklahoma, April 1936. Photo by Rothstein

In the water-cut gullies the earth dusted down in dry little streams. ...And as the sharp sun struck day after day, the leaves of the young corn became less stiff and erect; they bent in a curve at first, and then, as the central ribs of strength grew weak, each leaf tilted downward. Then it was June, and the sun shone more fiercely. The brown lines on the corn leaves widened and moved in on the central ribs. The weeds frayed and edged back toward their roots. The air was thin and the sky more pale; and every day the earth paled.

In the roads where the teams moved, where the wheels milled the ground and the hooves of the horses beat the ground, the dirt crust and the dust formed. Every moving thing lifted the dust in the air: a walking man lifted a thin layer as high as his waist, and a wagon lifted the dust as high as the fence tops, and an automobile boiled a cloud behind it....

The dawn came, but no day. In the gray sky a red sun appeared, a dim red circle that gave a little light, like dusk; and as that day advanced, the dusk slipped back toward darkness, and the wind cried and whimpered over the fallen corn.

Men and women huddled in their houses, and they tied handkerchiefs over their noses when they went out, and wore goggles to protect their eyes.

When the night came again it was black night, for the stars could not pierce the dust to get down, and the window lights could not even spread beyond their own yards. Now the dust was evenly mixed with air, an emulsion of dust and air. Houses were shut tight, and cloth wedged around doors and windows, but the dust came in so thinly that it could not be seen in the air, and it settled like pollen on the tables and chairs, on the dishes. The people brushed it from the shoulders. Little lines of dust lay at the door sills.

Grasshoppers and Dust

Ruth Loriks, wife of a farmer and State Senator from South Dakota, was interviewed by Studs Terkel. She described the grasshoppers that ravished the farms.

Source: Studs Terkel, *Hard Times* (Pantheon Books, New York: 1970).

One time we were driving up to Aberdeen. It was during the grasshopper days in 1933. The sun was shining brightly when we left home. When we were about half way, it just turned dark. It was the grasshoppers that covered the sun. We had a large garden. The chickens would go in there and pick what little grass which they'd find. Our neighbors said: "The grasshoppers have come in, they'd taken every leaf off our trees, they're even starting to eat the fence posts." I thought that was a joke. Well, the next day they moved on here, and they did line up the fence posts. My faithful hen sort of kept them off the tomatoes, but they were moving in.

One day at noon, we had one of our worst dust storms. I never want to see one again. We could just see it float in, and we had good, heavy storm windows....

This neighbor woman lost her husband, and, of course, he was owing in the bank. So the auctioneers come out there, and she served lunch, and she stood weeping in the windows. "There goes our last cow...." And the horses, she called 'em by names. It just pretty near broke our hearts. They didn't give her a chance to take care of her bills. They never gave her an offer. They just came and cleared it out. And she stood there crying.

Searching For Hope

The Country Migrates

In the study of unemployment in the United States in the midst of the depression, Fortune *reported some of the social "curiosities," most notably the migration of unemployed people.*

Source: *Fortune* Magazine, September, 1932.

[T] he depression, along with its misery, has produced its social curiosities, not the least of which is the wandering population it has spilled on the roads. Means of locomotion vary but the objective is always the same—somewhere else. No one has yet undertaken to estimate the number of hitch-hikers whose thumbs jerk onward along the American pike, nor the number of spavined Fords dragging destitute families from town to town in search of a solvent relative or a generous friend. But the total migratory population of the country has been put at 600,000 to 1,000,000. The Pacific Coast, the Southwest, and the Atlantic South are the habitat of the larger groups. Los Angeles once had over 70,000 with a daily influx of 1,500 more while the state of California reported an increase of 311.8 per cent in the monthly average of meals served to homeless men in early 1931 as compared with early 1929. And 365 vagrant boys running from fourteen to twenty and including college students, high school students, and eighth-graders applied to the Salt Lake Salvation Army and the Salt Lake County Jail for shelter between May 15 and June 15, 1932. Many of them were homeless, destitute children of families broken up by unemployment. [A]lmost all of them were traveling alone or with one companion....

A family of migratory fruit workers from Tennessee, camped out in a field near the packing house in Winter Haven, Florida, January 1937. Photo by Rothstein

The presence of these wandering groups is curious and significant....When millions of people have no relation to the land and are able at the same time to find cheap transportation, the effect of an economic crisis is not to fix them in one place but to drive them elsewhere. And the consequence, as regards these groups, is complete failure of local relief. The destitute families of the Fords and the homeless men of the flat cars [railroad freight trains] are entitled to relief in no city.